FOR ORGANS, PIANOS & ELECTRONIC KEYBOARDS

63

Classical Music
2nd Edition

BEETHOVEN

DEBUSSY

TCHAIKOVSKY

MOZART

J.S. BACH

CHOPIN

BRAHMS

WAGNER

LULLY

ISBN 978-1-5400-2973-7

Hal•Leonard®
7777 W. Bluemound Rd. P.O. Box 13819 Milwaukee, WI 53213

In Australia Contact:
Hal Leonard Australia Pty. Ltd.
4 Lentara Court
Cheltenham, Victoria, 3192 Australia
Email: ausadmin@halleonard.com.au

Copyright © 2018 by HAL LEONARD LLC
International Copyright Secured   All Rights Reserved

For all works contained herein:
Unauthorized copying, arranging, adapting, recording, Internet posting, public performance,
or other distribution of the printed music in this publication is an infringement of copyright.
Infringers are liable under the law.

E-Z Play® Today Music Notation © 1975 by HAL LEONARD LLC
E-Z PLAY and EASY ELECTRONIC KEYBOARD MUSIC are registered trademarks of HAL LEONARD LLC.

Visit Hal Leonard Online at
www.halleonard.com

T0057402

 **Registration Guide**

- Match the Registration number on the song to the corresponding numbered category below. Select and activate an instrumental sound available on your instrument.

- Choose an automatic rhythm appropriate to the mood and style of the song. (Consult your Owner's Guide for proper operation of automatic rhythm features.)

- Adjust the tempo and volume controls to comfortable settings.

Registration

1	Mellow	Flutes, Clarinet, Oboe, Flugel Horn, Trombone, French Horn, Organ Flutes
2	Ensemble	Brass Section, Sax Section, Wind Ensemble, Full Organ, Theater Organ
3	Strings	Violin, Viola, Cello, Fiddle, String Ensemble, Pizzicato, Organ Strings
4	Guitars	Acoustic/Electric Guitars, Banjo, Mandolin, Dulcimer, Ukulele, Hawaiian Guitar
5	Mallets	Vibraphone, Marimba, Xylophone, Steel Drums, Bells, Celesta, Chimes
6	Liturgical	Pipe Organ, Hand Bells, Vocal Ensemble, Choir, Organ Flutes
7	Bright	Saxophones, Trumpet, Mute Trumpet, Synth Leads, Jazz/Gospel Organs
8	Piano	Piano, Electric Piano, Honky Tonk Piano, Harpsichord, Clavi
9	Novelty	Melodic Percussion, Wah Trumpet, Synth, Whistle, Kazoo, Perc. Organ
10	Bellows	Accordion, French Accordion, Mussette, Harmonica, Pump Organ, Bagpipes

Andante cantabile
from SYMPHONY NO. 5

Registration 8
Rhythm: Fox Trot

By Pyotr Il'yich Tchaikovsky

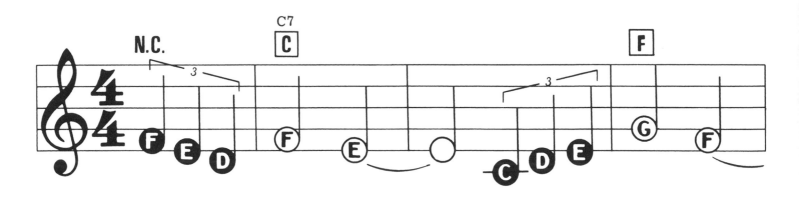

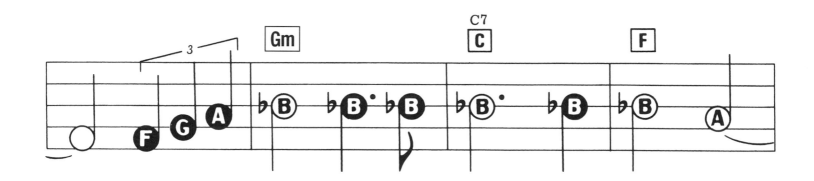

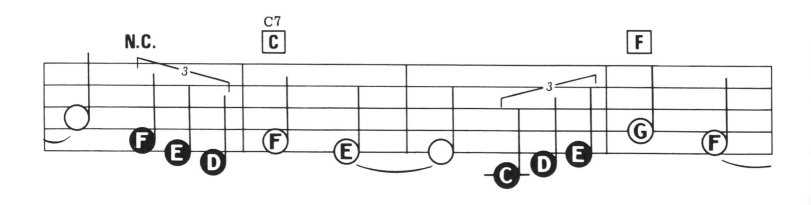

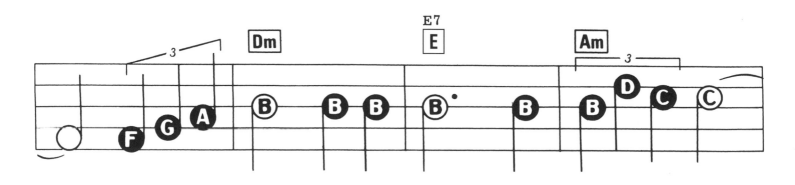

Copyright © 1975 by HAL LEONARD CORPORATION
International Copyright Secured   All Rights Reserved

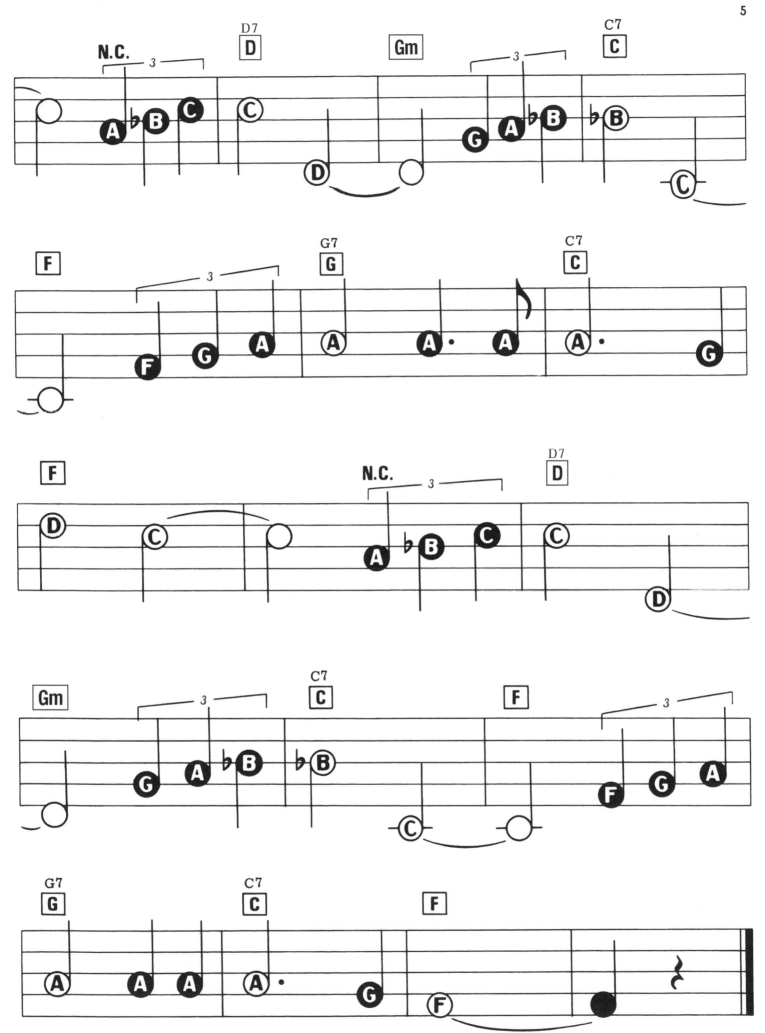

Barcarolle
from THE TALES OF HOFFMANN

Registration 1
Rhythm: Waltz

By Jacques Offenbach

Copyright © 2014 by HAL LEONARD CORPORATION
International Copyright Secured   All Rights Reserved

Dance of the Hours
from LA GIOCONDA

Registration 5
Rhythm: Fox Trot

By Amilcare Ponchielli

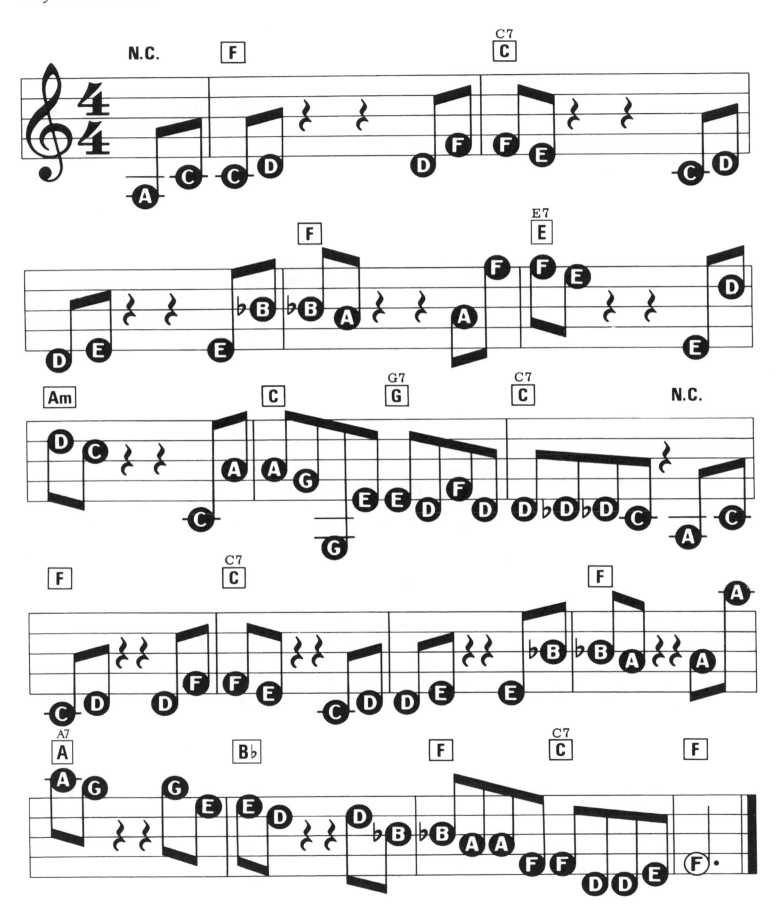

Copyright © 1977 by HAL LEONARD CORPORATION
International Copyright Secured   All Rights Reserved

Clair de Lune
from SUITE BERGAMASQUE

Registration 8
Rhythm: Waltz or None

By Claude Debussy

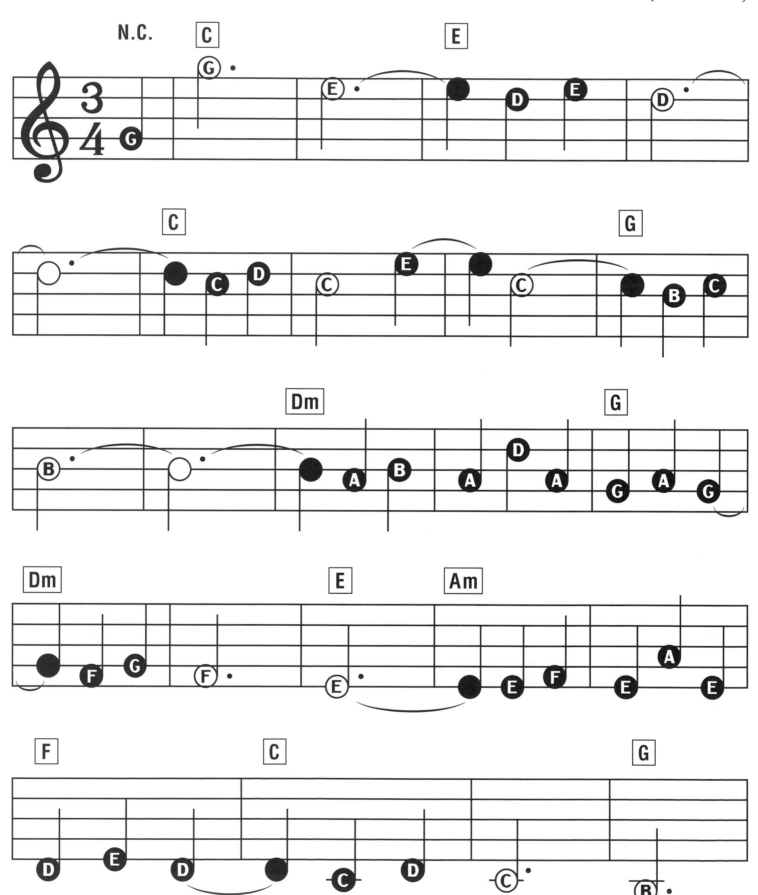

Copyright © 2014 by HAL LEONARD CORPORATION
International Copyright Secured   All Rights Reserved

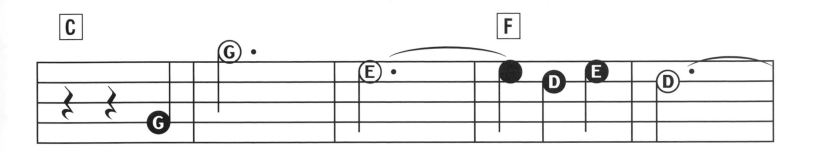

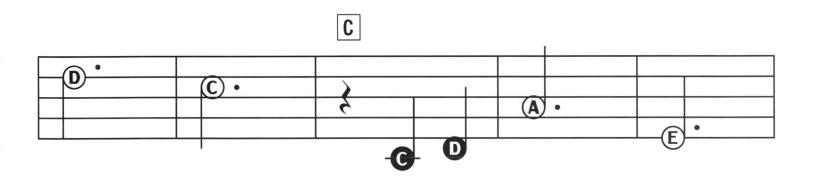

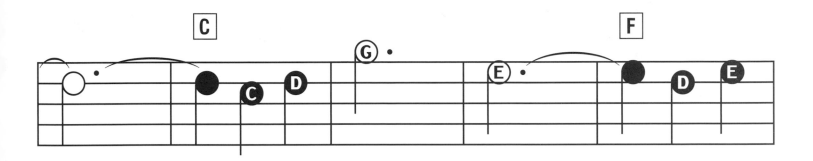

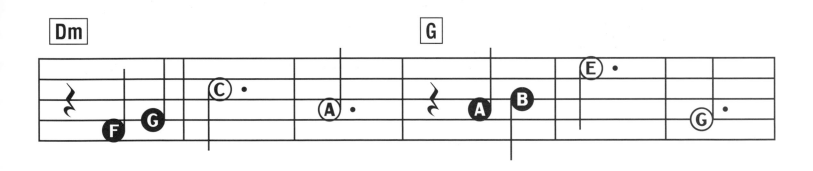

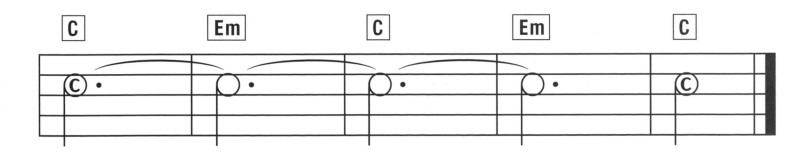

Coppelia Waltz

Registration 3
Rhythm: Waltz

By Léo Delibes

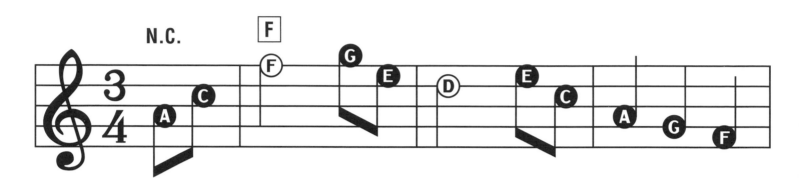

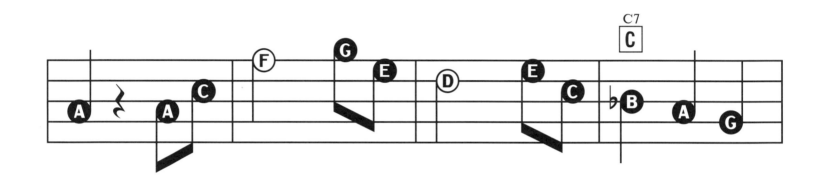

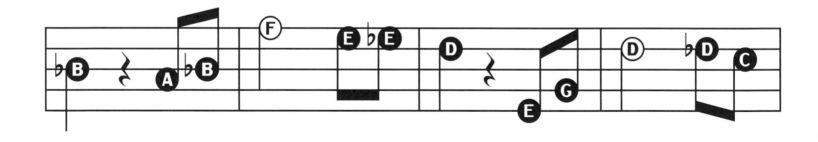

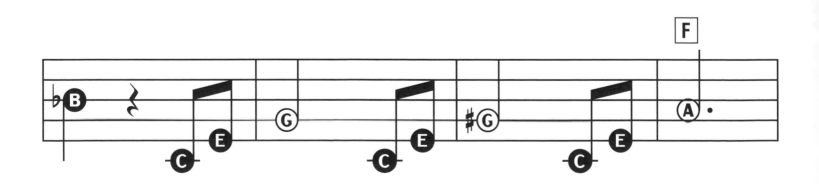

Copyright © 2018 by HAL LEONARD LLC
International Copyright Secured   All Rights Reserved

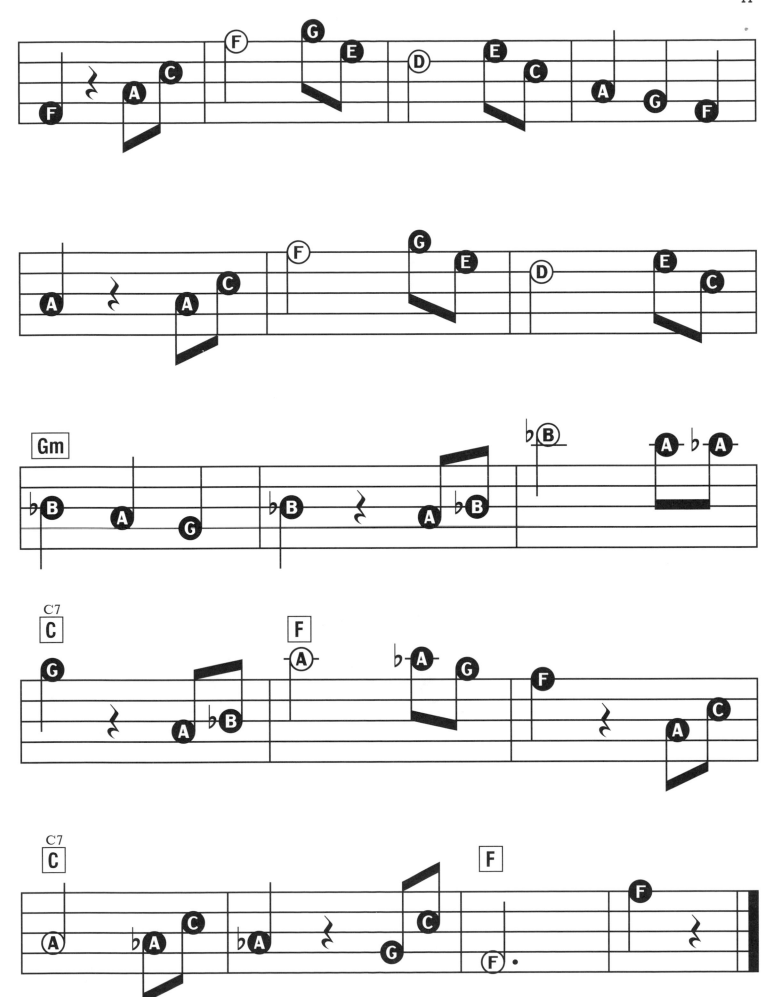

Danube Waves

Registration 8
Rhythm: Waltz

By Iosif Ivanovici

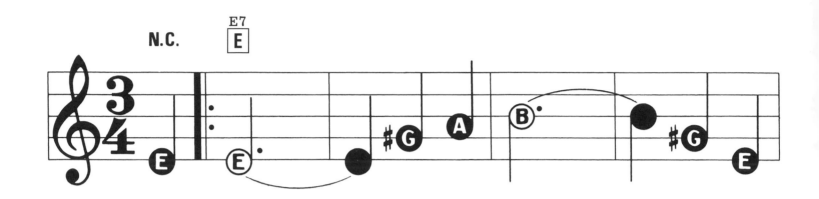

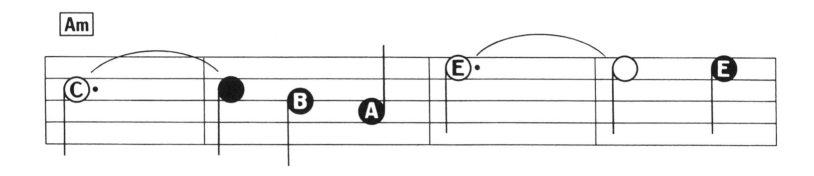

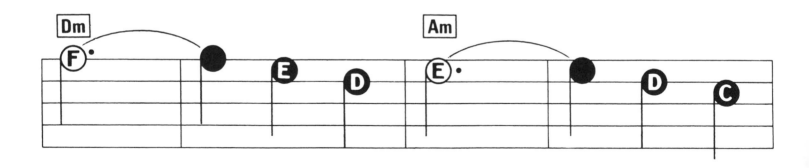

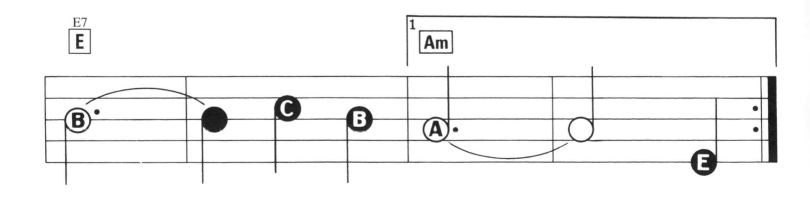

Copyright © 1977 by HAL LEONARD CORPORATION
International Copyright Secured   All Rights Reserved

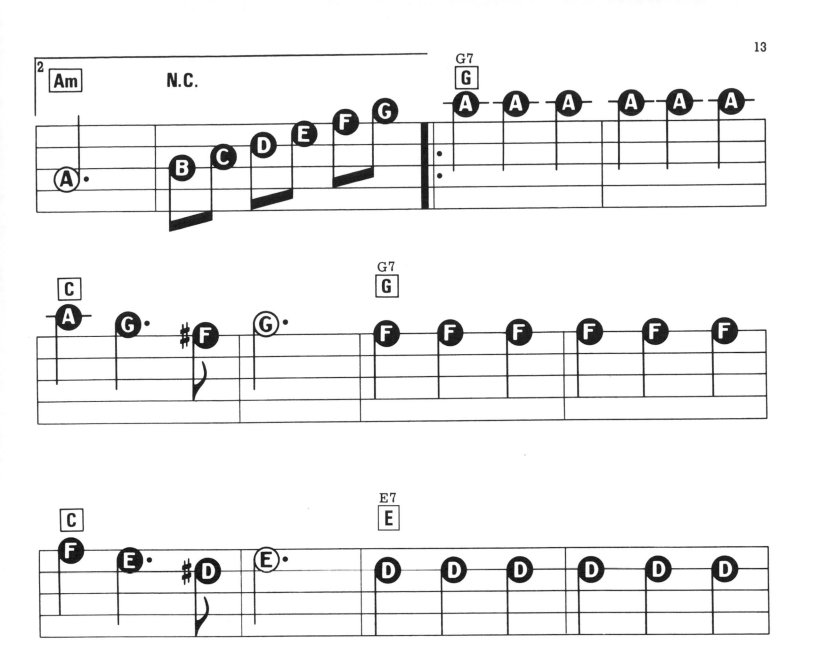

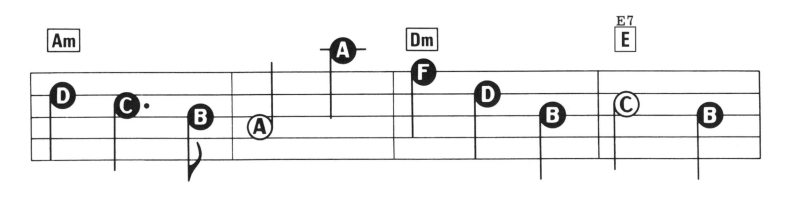

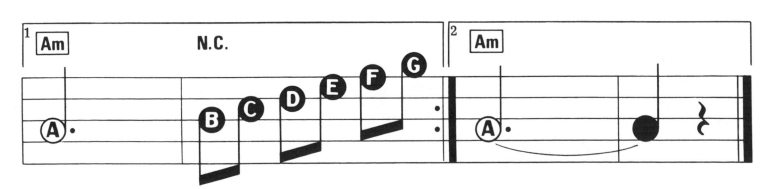

Hungarian Dance No. 5

Registration 3
Rhythm: Fox Trot

By Johannes Brahms

Copyright © 2018 by HAL LEONARD CORPORATION LLC
International Copyright Secured All Rights Reserved

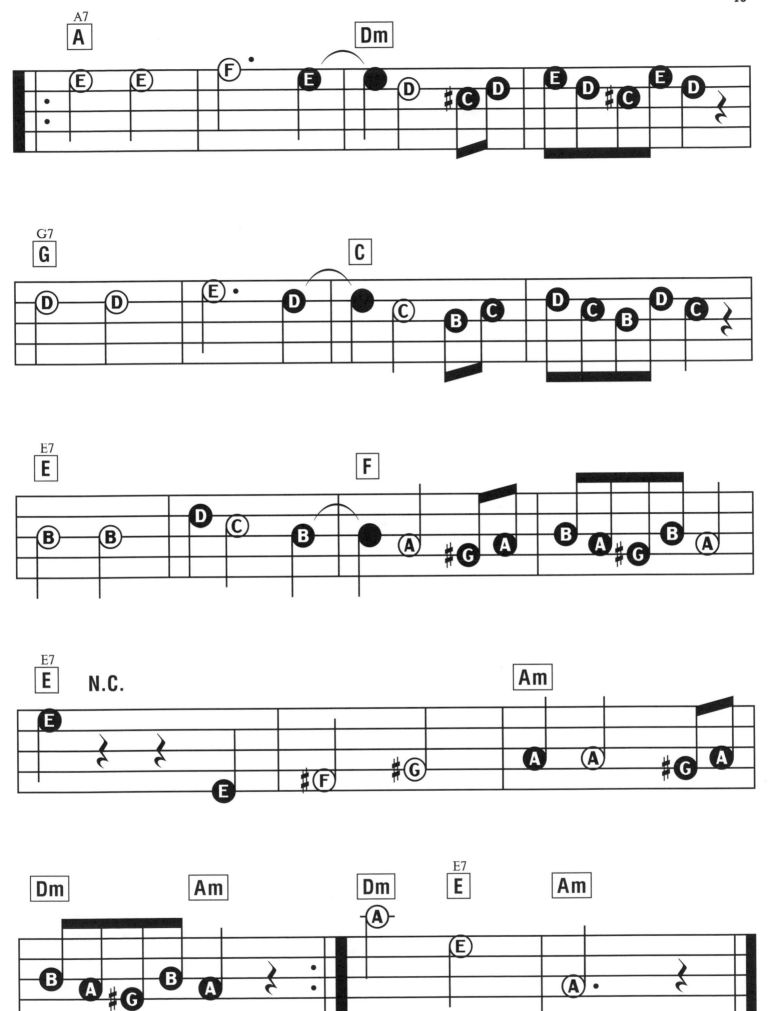

Intermezzo
from CAVALLERIA RUSTICANA

Registration 3
Rhythm: Waltz or None

By Pietro Mascagni

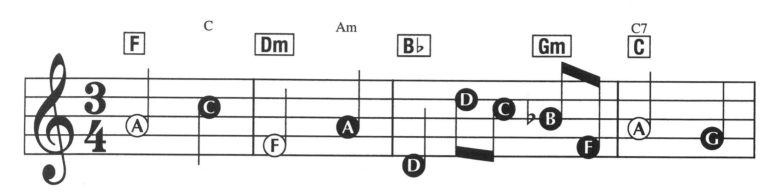

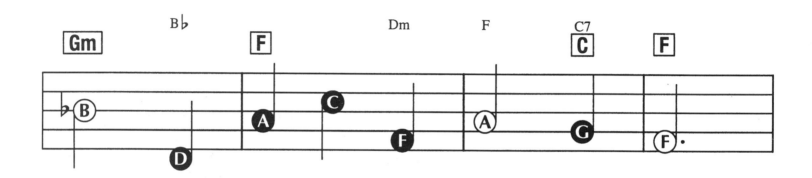

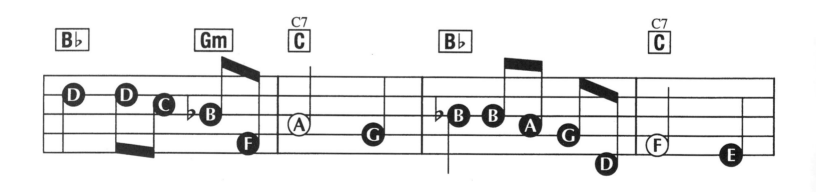

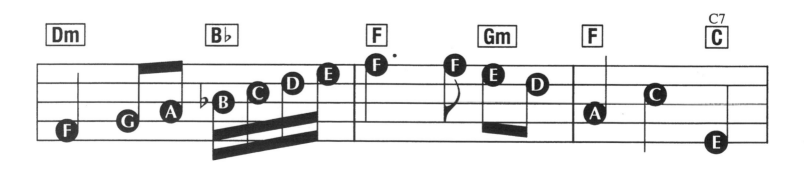

Copyright © 1994 by HAL LEONARD CORPORATION
International Copyright Secured   All Rights Reserved

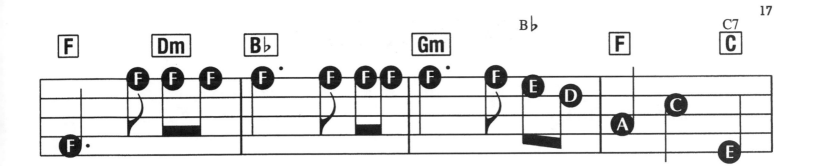

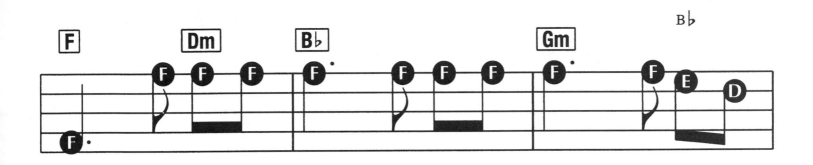

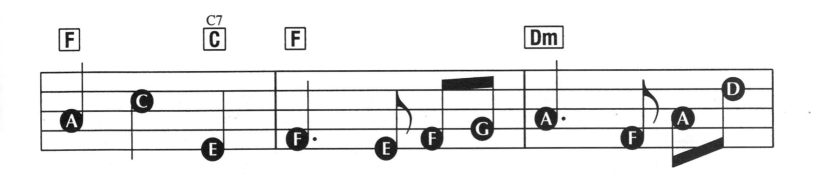

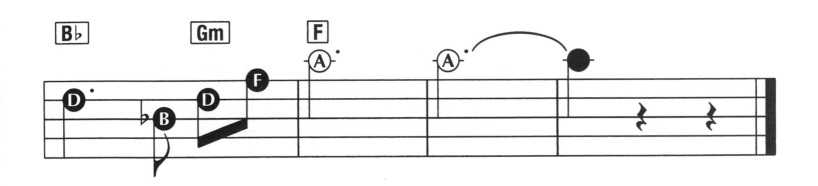

Melody in F

Registration 8
Rhythm: Ballad or Fox Trot

By Anton Rubinstein

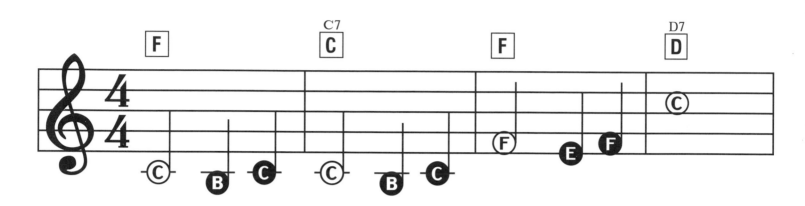

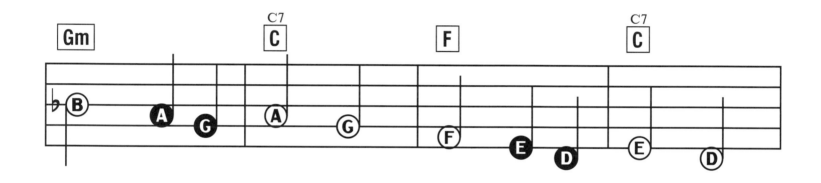

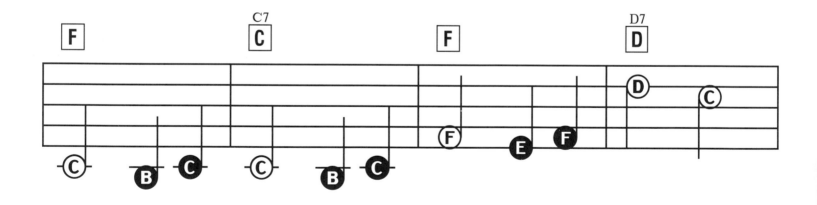

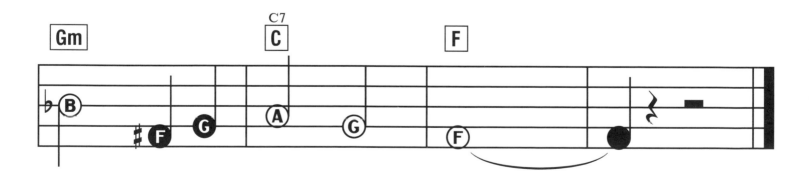

Copyright © 2018 by HAL LEONARD LLC
International Copyright Secured   All Rights Reserved

The Merry Widow Waltz
from THE MERRY WIDOW

Registration 3
Rhythm: Waltz

Words by Adrian Ross
Music by Franz Lehár

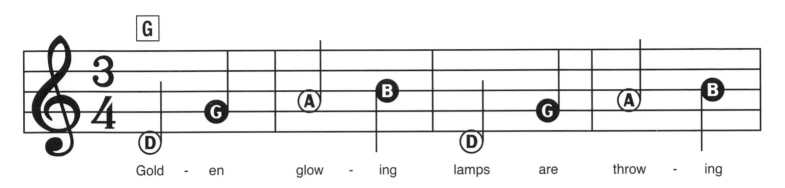

Gold - en   glow - ing   lamps are   throw - ing

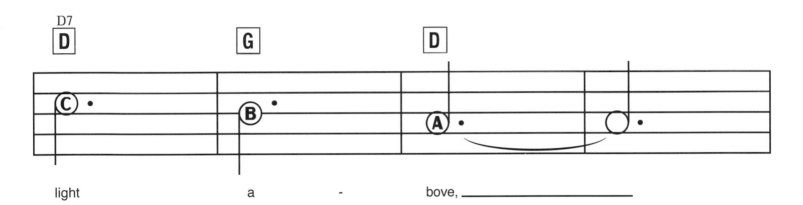

light   a -   bove, _____

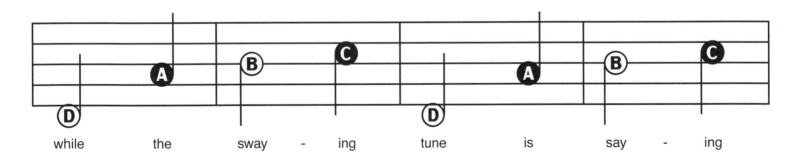

while   the   sway - ing   tune   is   say - ing

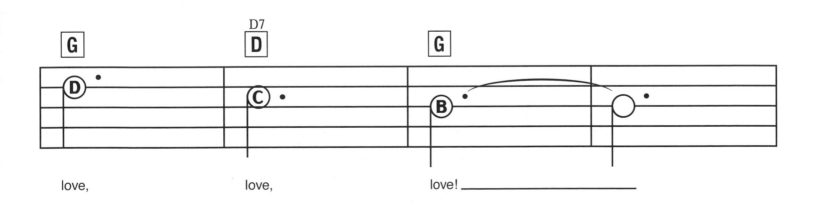

love,   love,   love! _____

Copyright © 2014 by HAL LEONARD CORPORATION
International Copyright Secured   All Rights Reserved

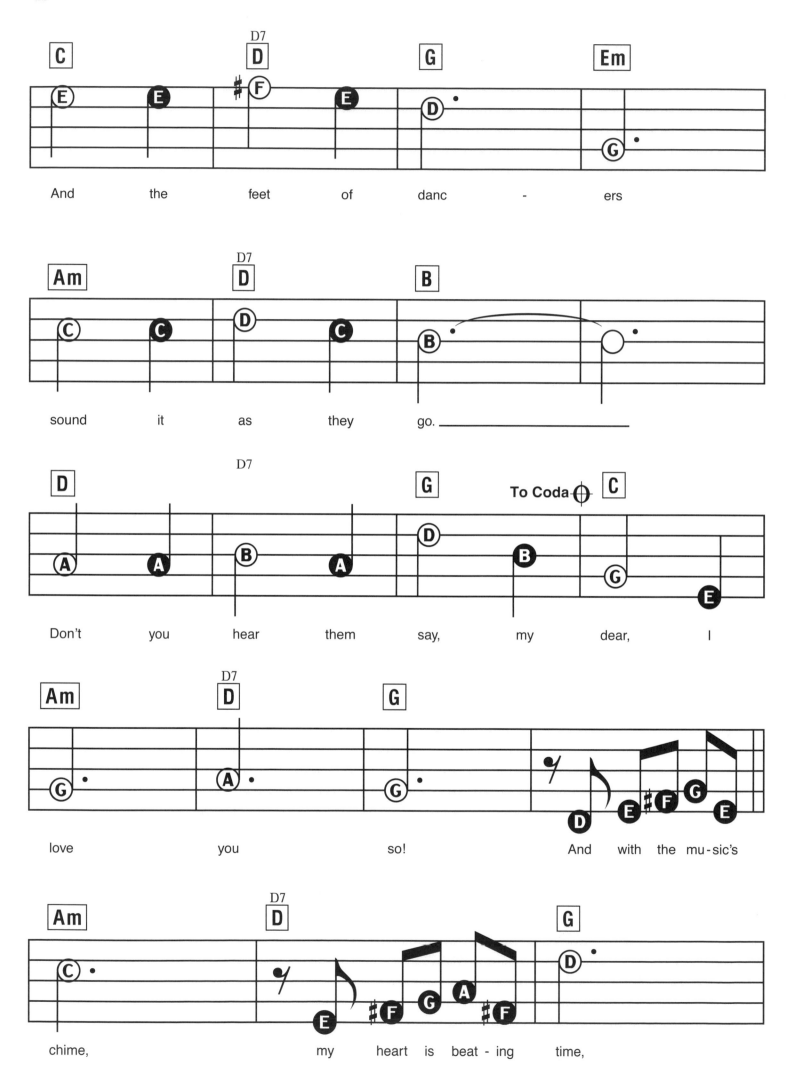

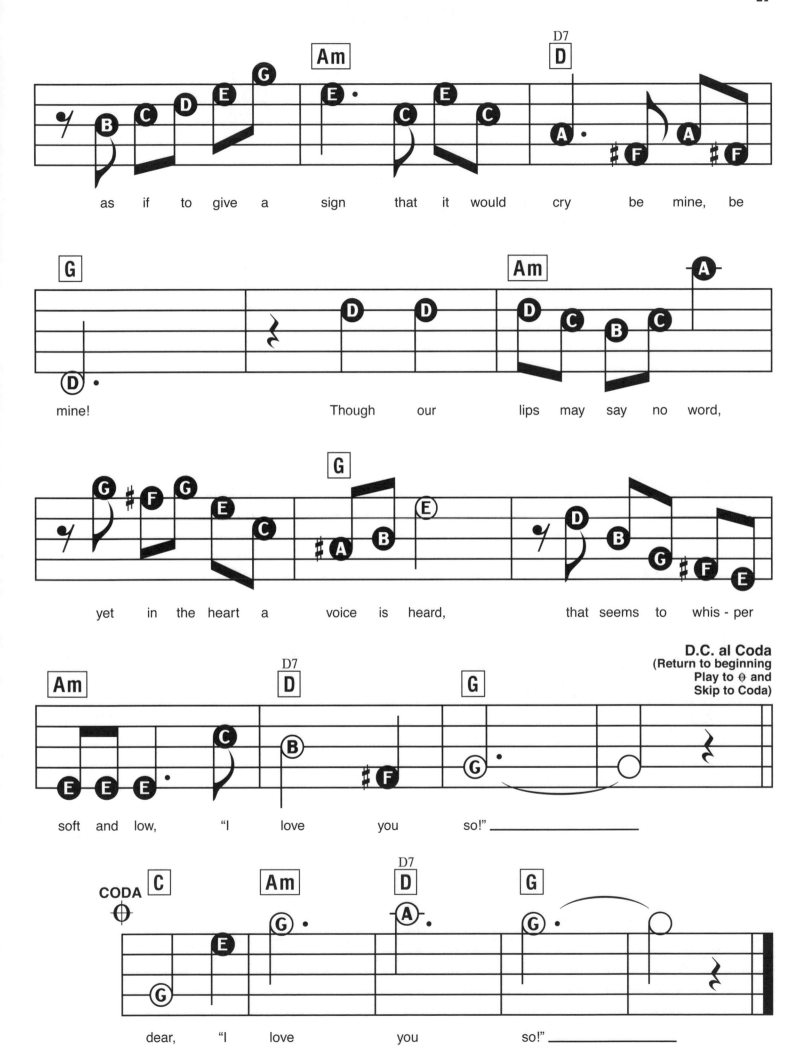

Minuet
from DON GIOVANNI

Registration 3
Rhythm: Waltz

By Wolfgang Amadeus Mozart

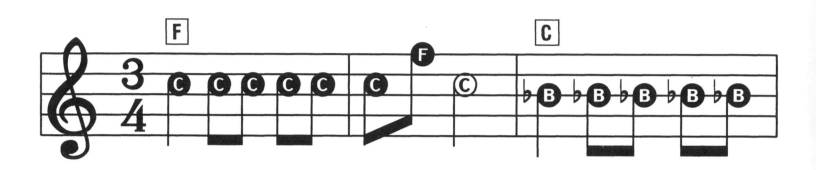

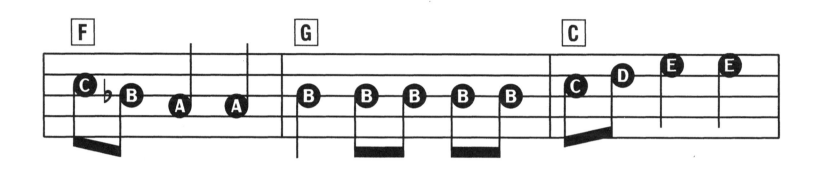

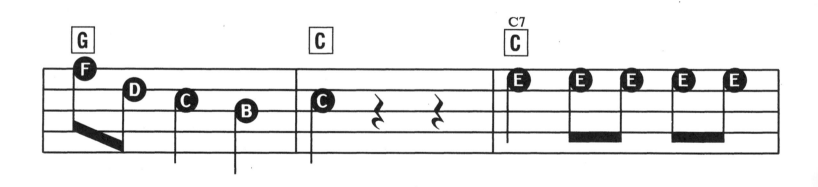

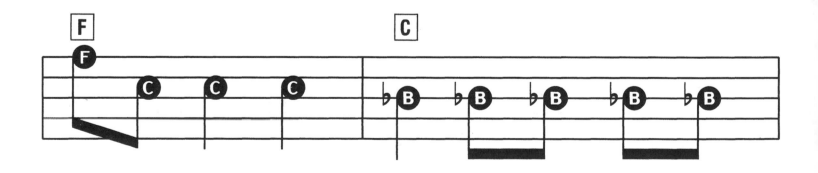

Copyright © 1992 by HAL LEONARD CORPORATION
International Copyright Secured   All Rights Reserved

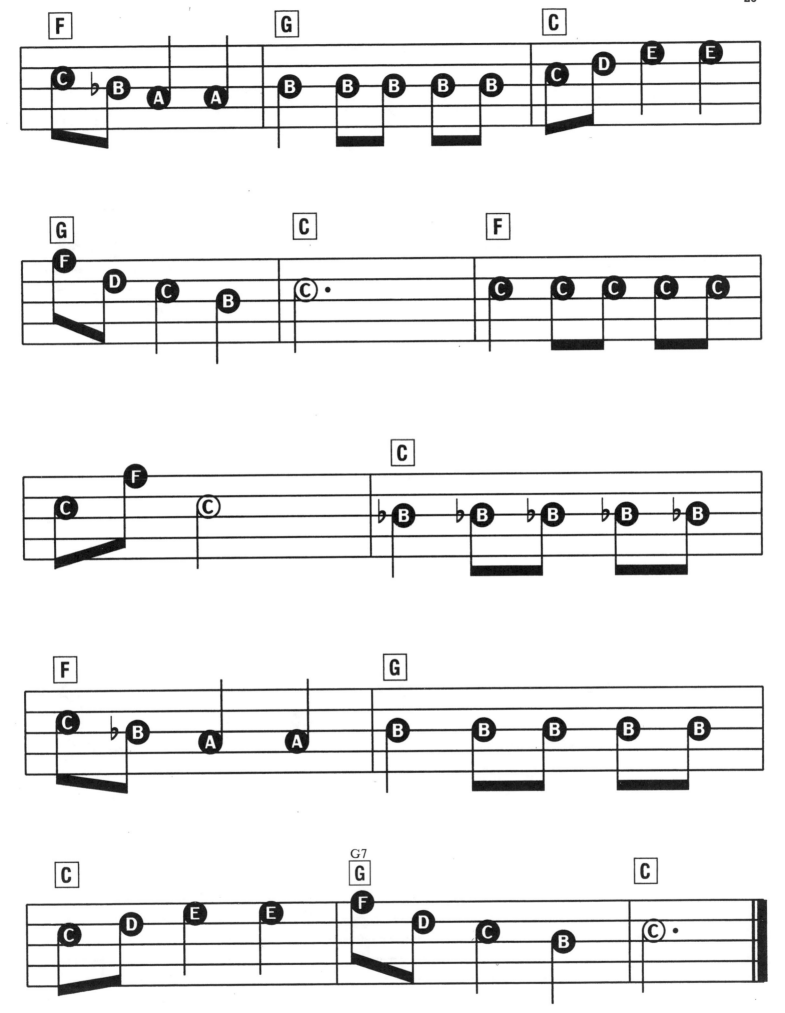

Pilgrims' Chorus
from TANNHÄUSER

Registration 6
Rhythm: Waltz

By Richard Wagner

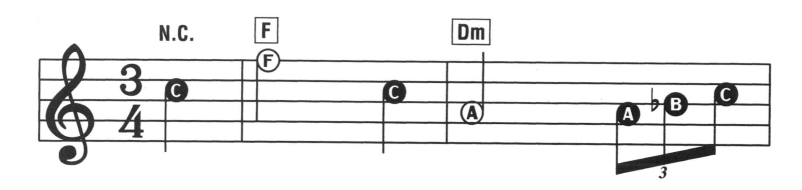

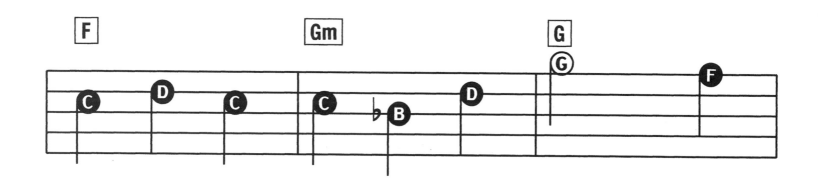

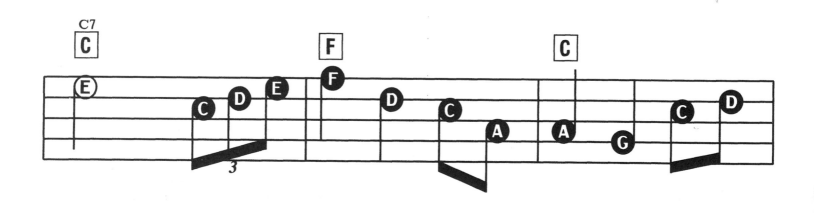

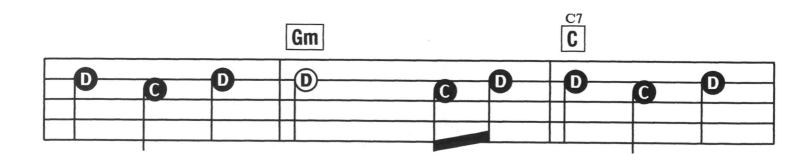

Copyright © 1992 by HAL LEONARD CORPORATION
International Copyright Secured   All Rights Reserved

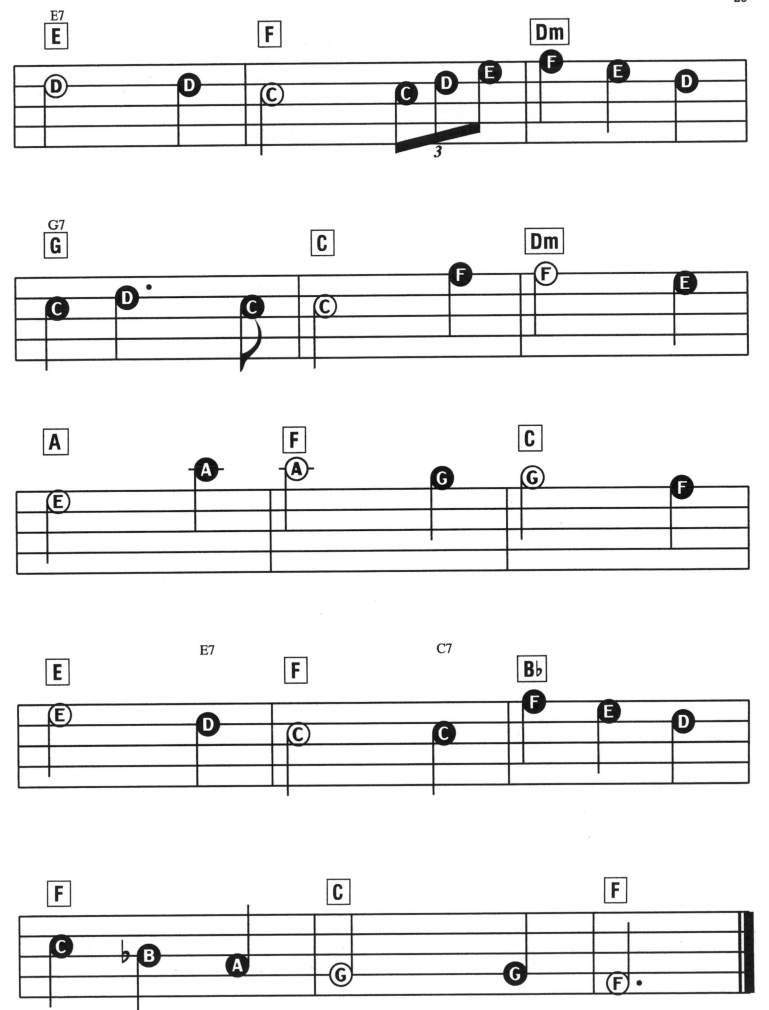

Polovetsian Dances
from PRINCE IGOR

Registration 3
Rhythm: Fox Trot or March

By Alexander Borodin

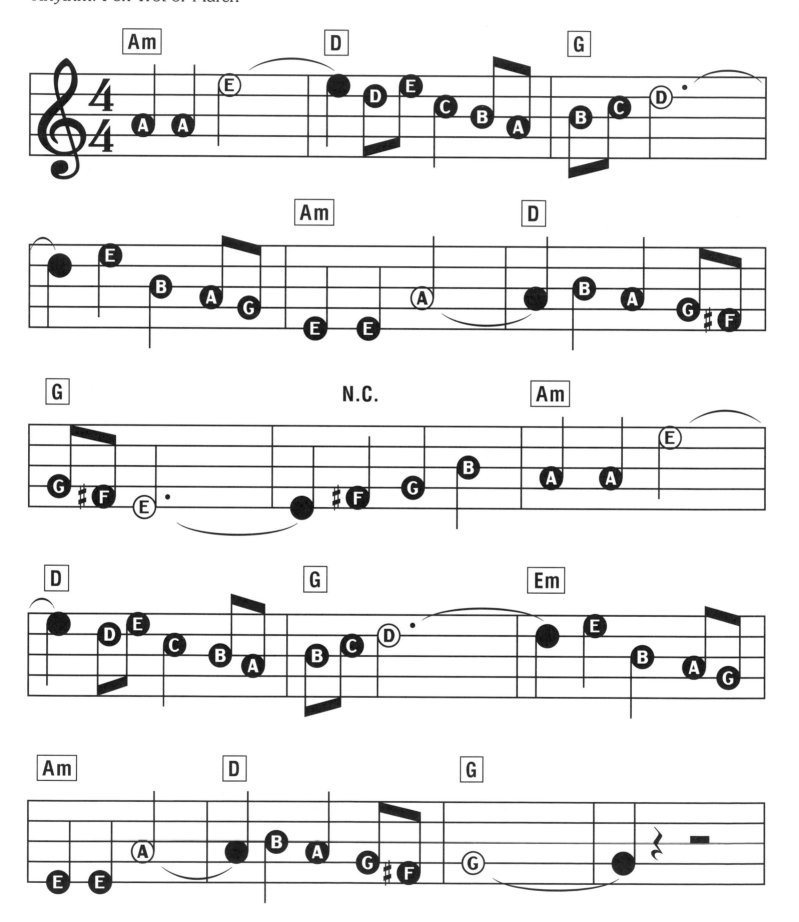

Copyright © 2004 by HAL LEONARD CORPORATION
International Copyright Secured   All Rights Reserved

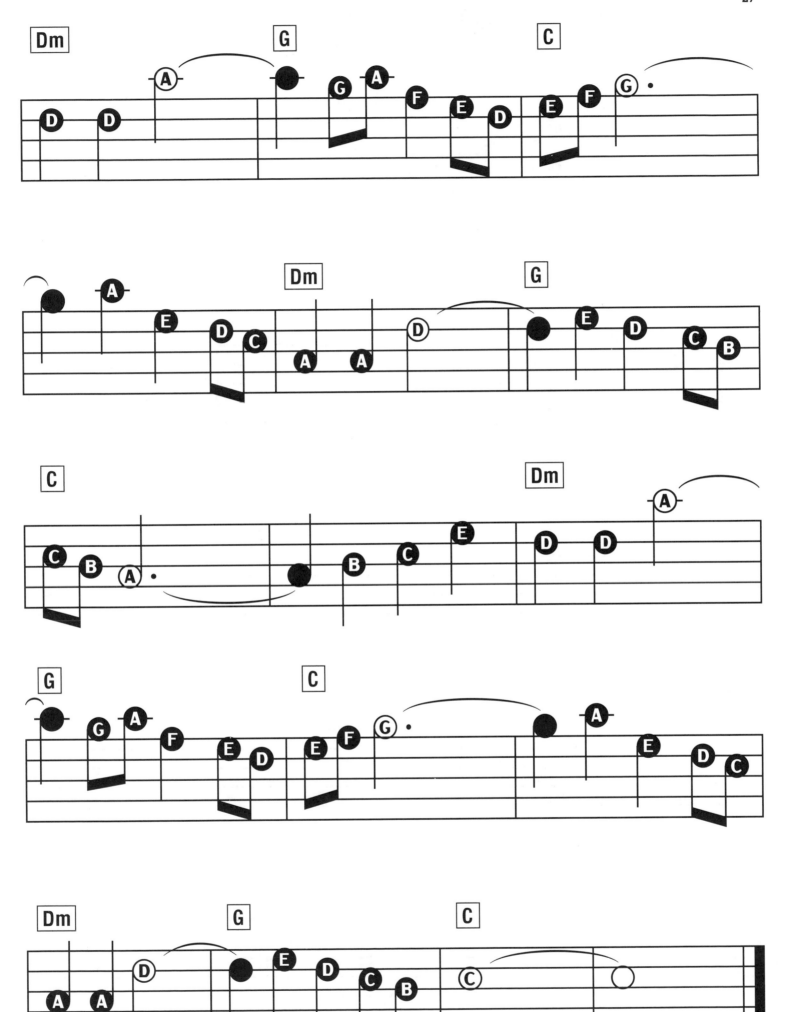

Ride of the Valkyries
from DIE WALKÜRE

Registration 2
Rhythm: Waltz

By Richard Wagner

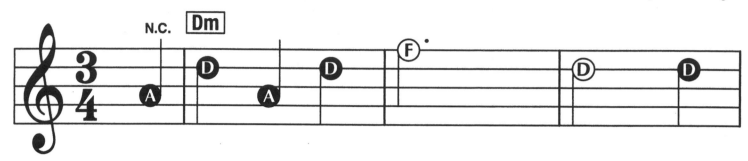

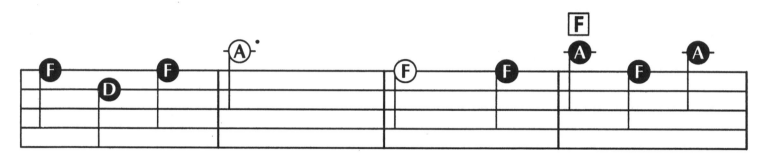

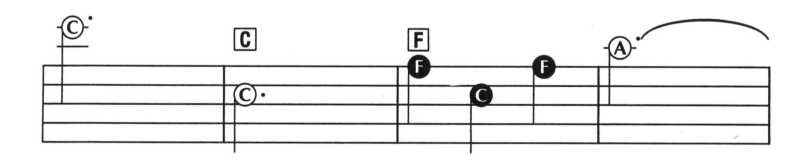

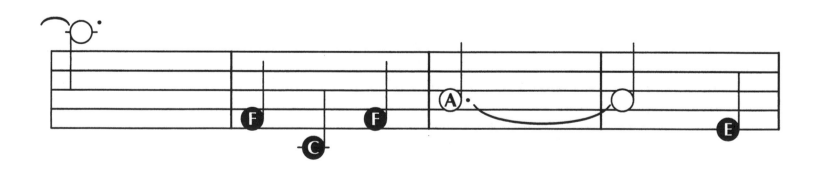

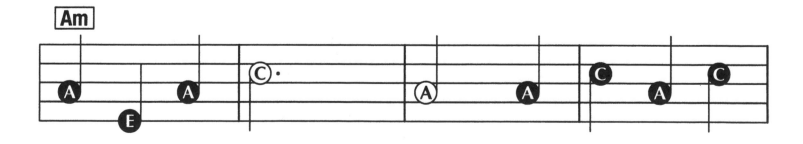

Copyright © 1992 by HAL LEONARD CORPORATION
International Copyright Secured   All Rights Reserved

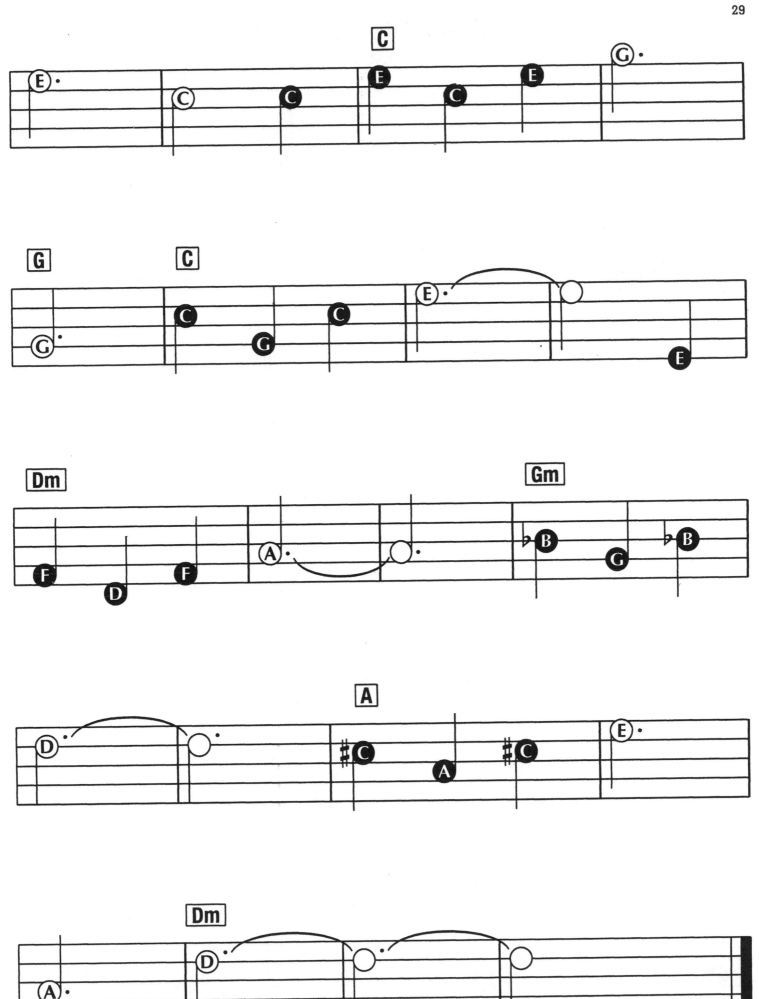

The Skaters
(Waltz)

Registration 5
Rhythm: Waltz

By Emil Waldteufer

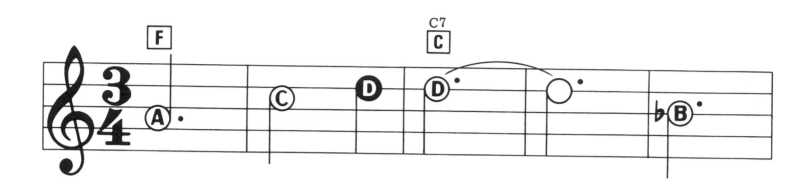

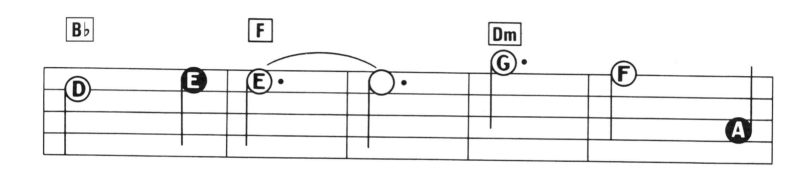

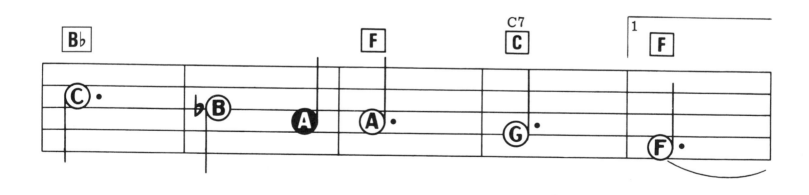

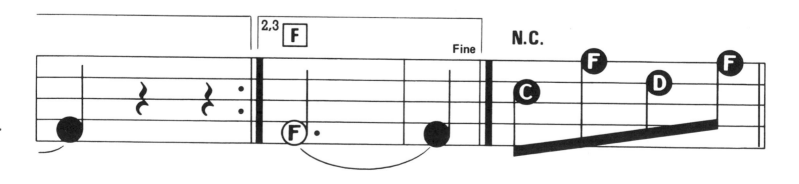

Copyright Copyright © 1975 by HAL LEONARD CORPORATION
International Copyright Secured   All Rights Reserved

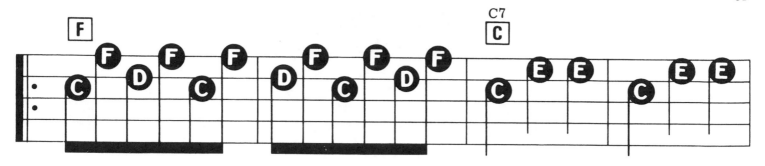

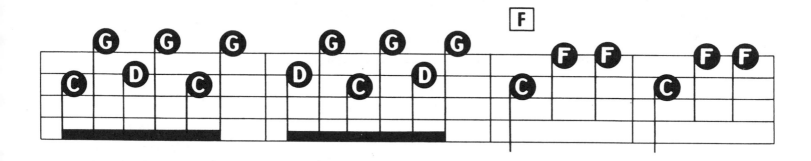

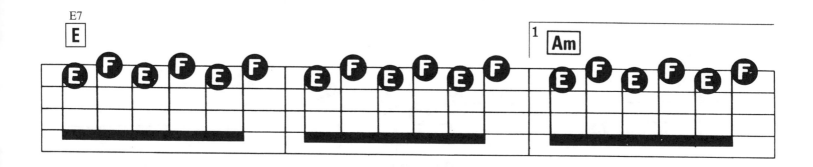

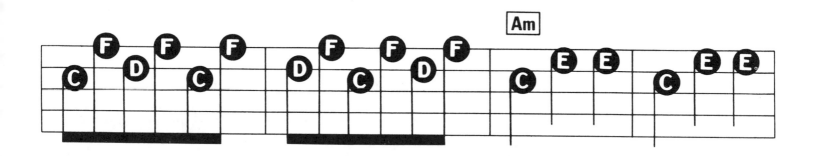

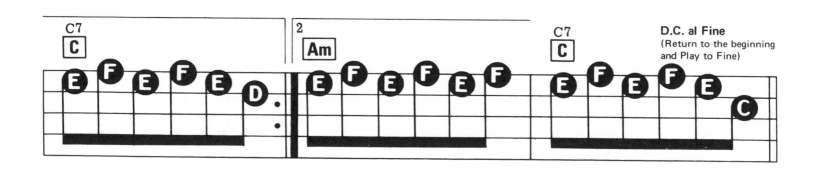

Spring
from THE FOUR SEASONS

Registration 3
Rhythm: March

By Antonio Vivaldi

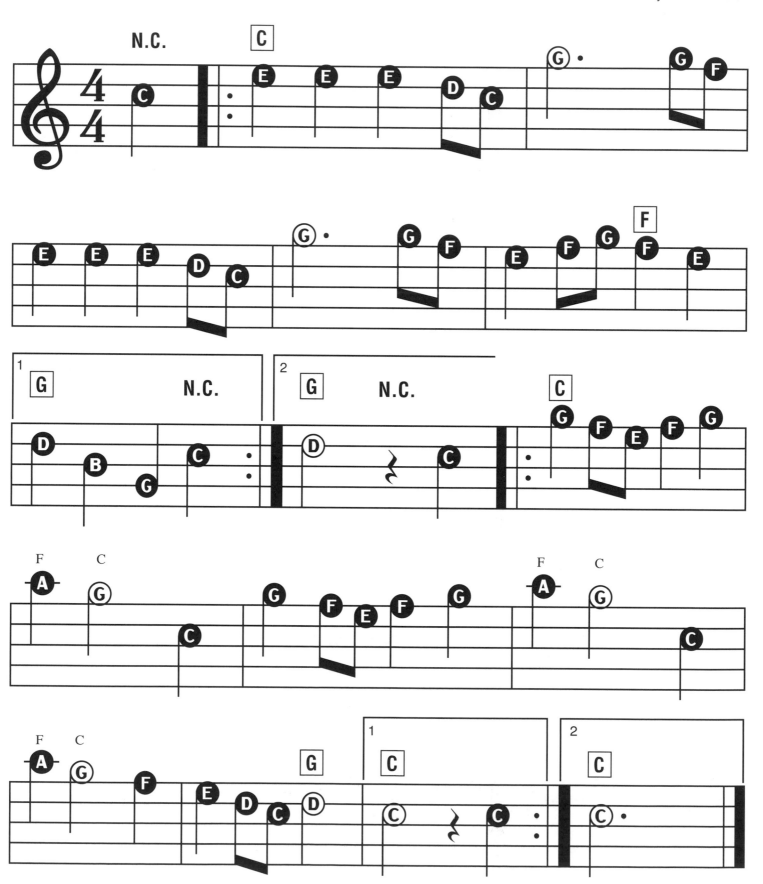

Copyright © 2018 by HAL LEONARD LLC
International Copyright Secured   All Rights Reserved

Symphony No. 40 in G Minor
First Movement (Molto allegro)

Registration 3
Rhythm: Fox Trot or None

By Wolfgang Amadeus Mozart

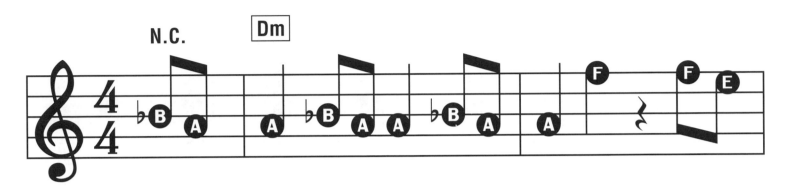

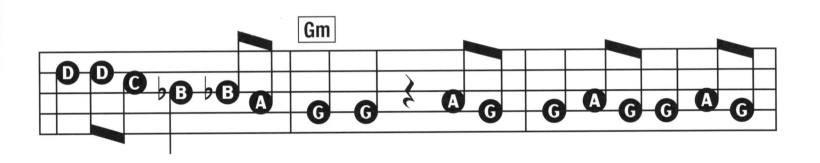

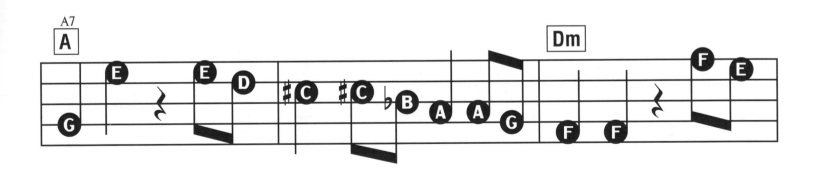

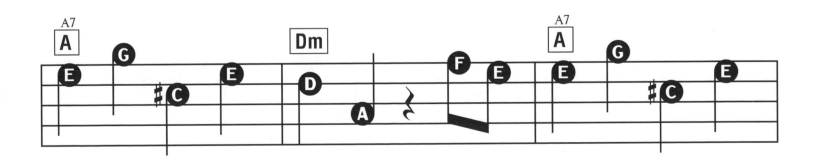

Copyright © 2015 by HAL LEONARD CORPORATION
International Copyright Secured   All Rights Reserved

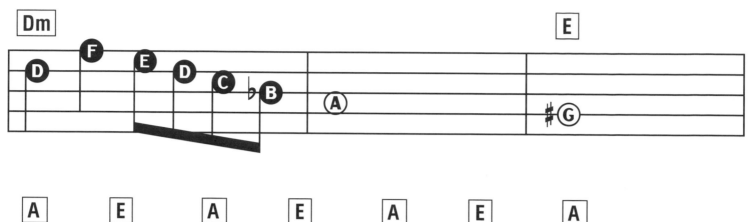

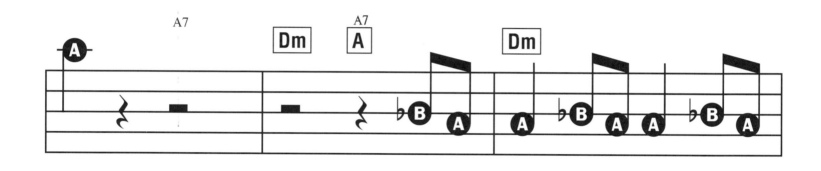

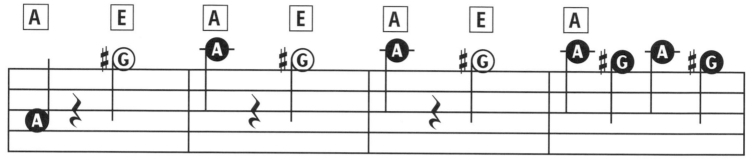

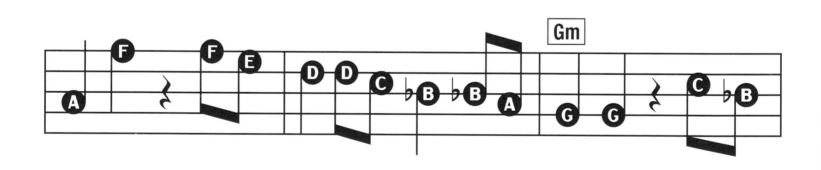

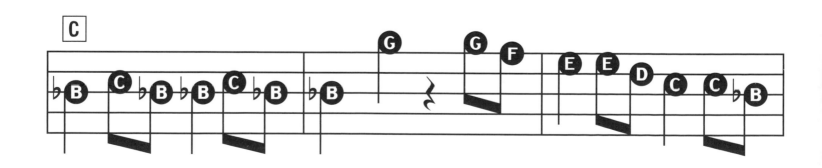

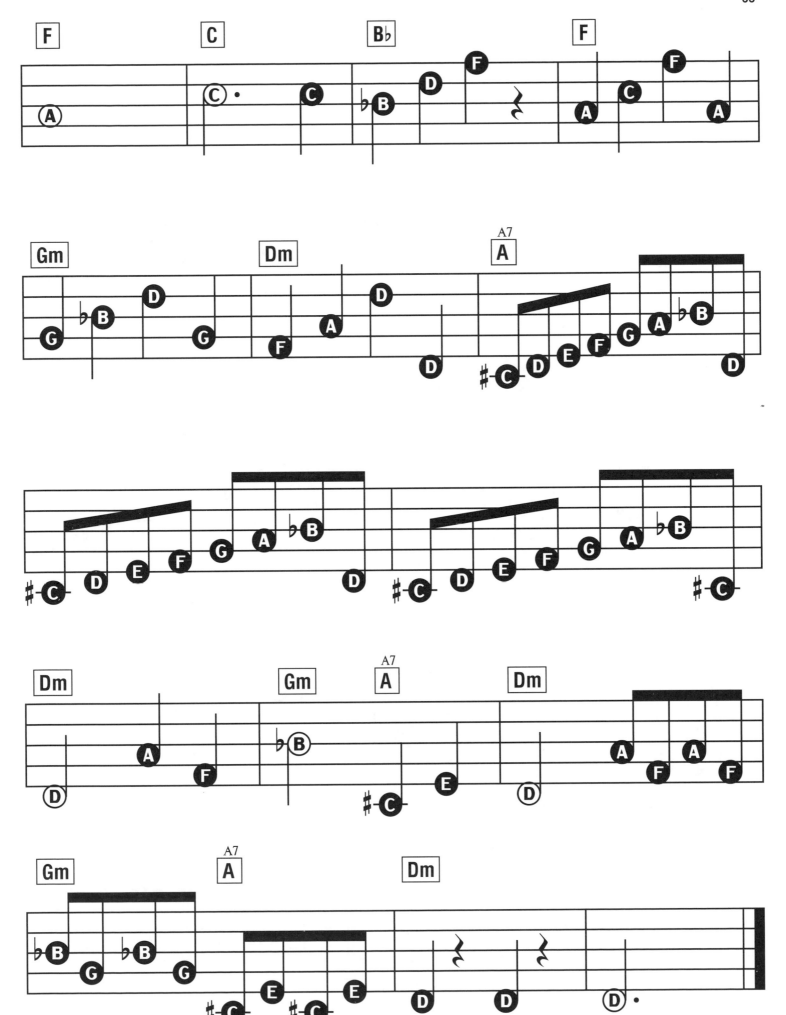

Toccata and Fugue in D Minor

Registration 6
Rhythm: None

By Johann Sebastian Bach

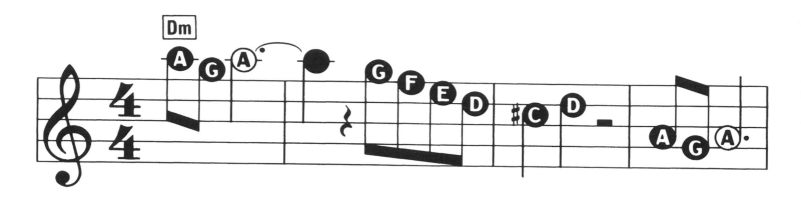

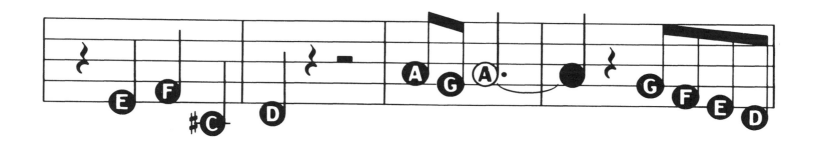

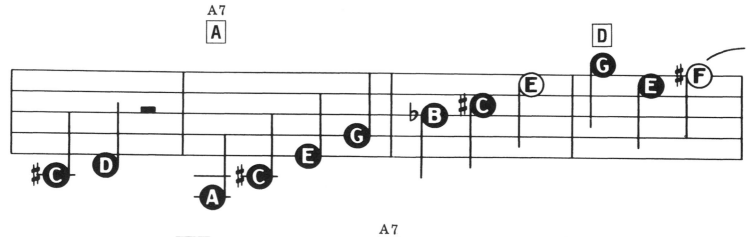

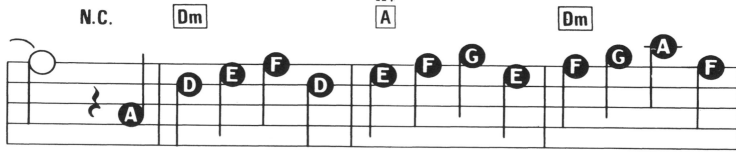

Copyright © 1980 by HAL LEONARD CORPORATION
International Copyright Secured   All Rights Reserved

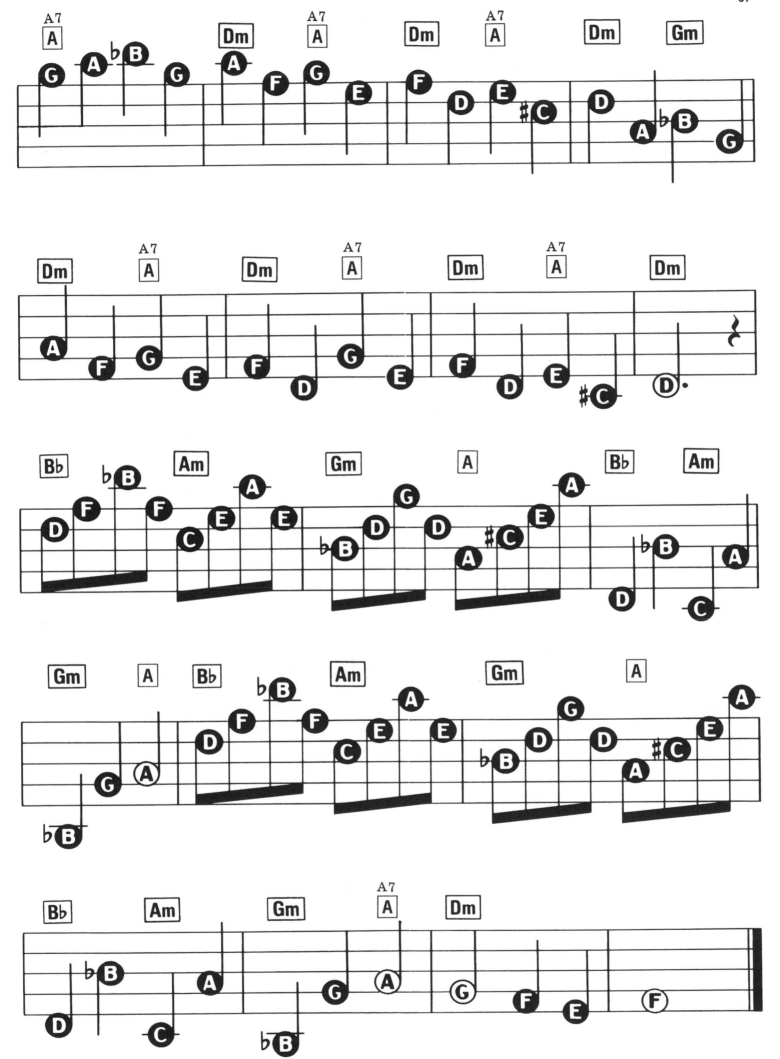

Triumphal March
from AIDA

Registration 2
Rhythm: March

By Giuseppe Verdi

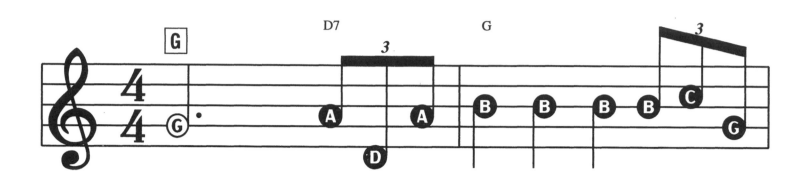

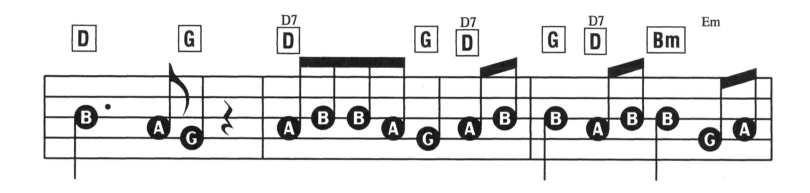

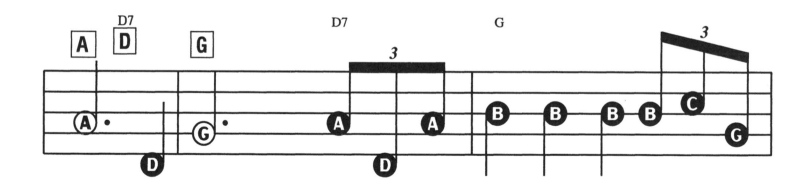

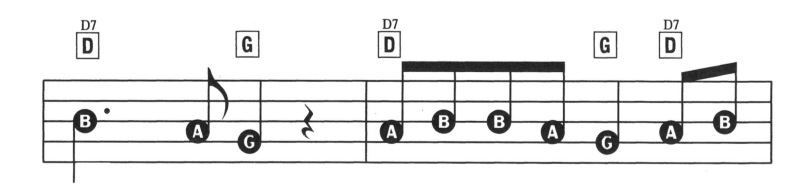

Copyright © 1992 by HAL LEONARD CORPORATION
International Copyright Secured   All Rights Reserved

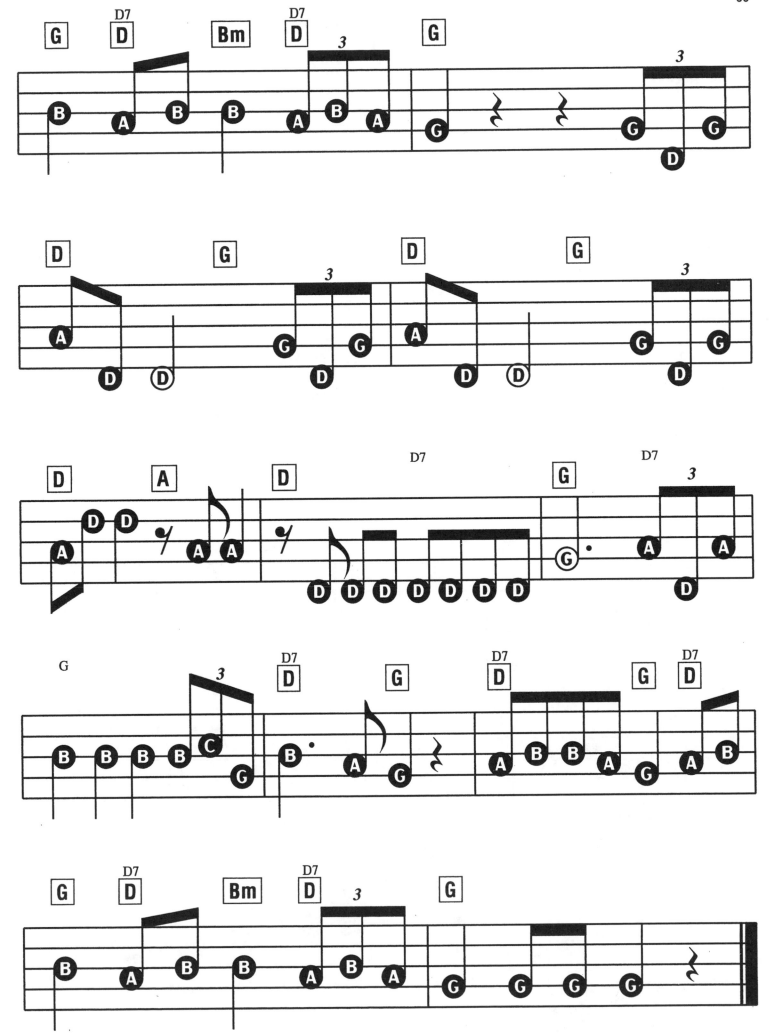

Trumpet Tune

Registration 6
Rhythm: March or None

By Jean-Baptiste Lully

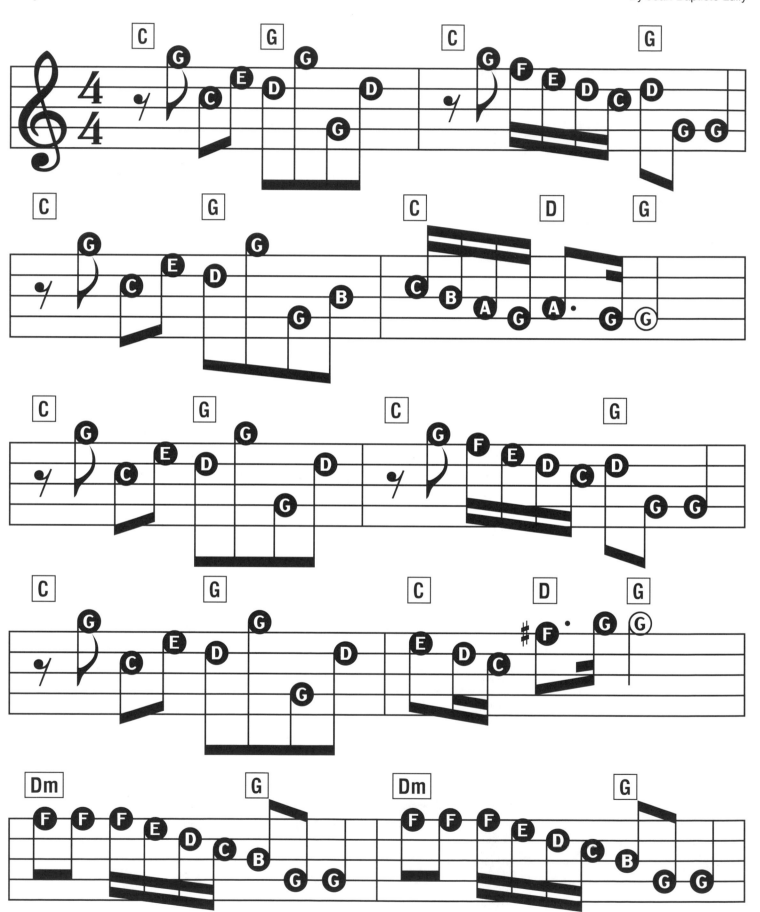

Copyright © 2014 by HAL LEONARD CORPORATION
International Copyright Secured   All Rights Reserved

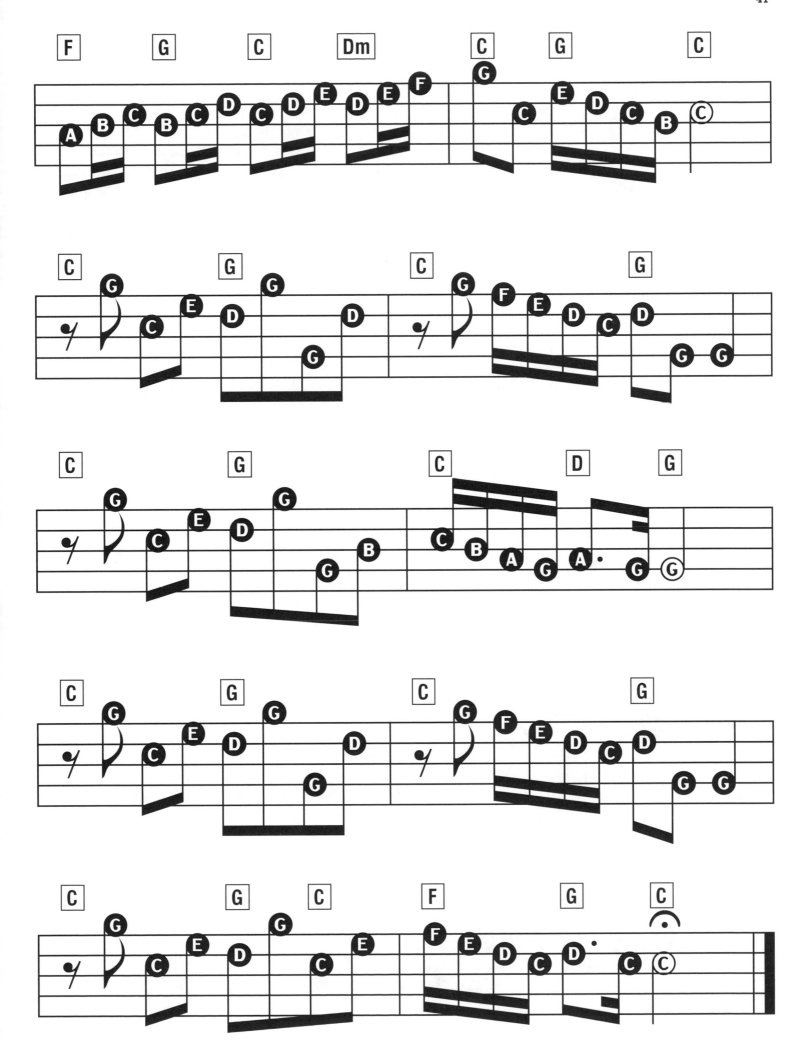

Turkish March
from THE RUINS OF ATHENS

Registration 5
Rhythm: March

By Ludwig van Beethoven

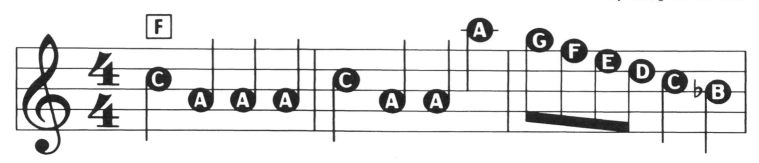

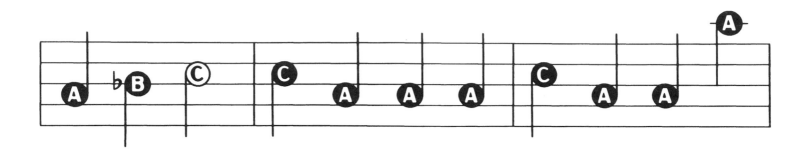

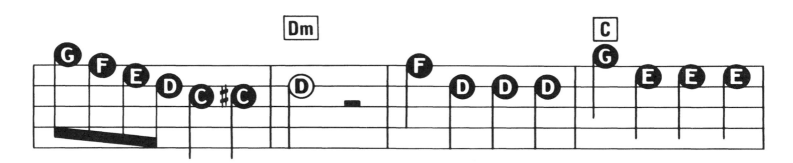

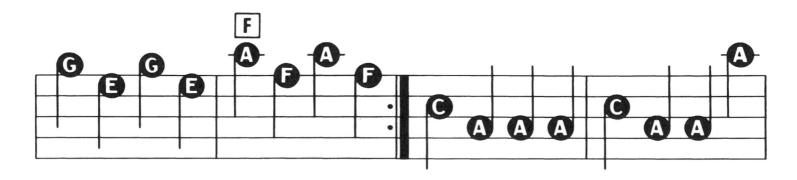

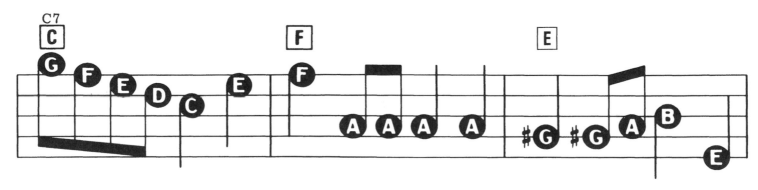

Copyright © 1980 by HAL LEONARD CORPORATION
International Copyright Secured   All Rights Reserved

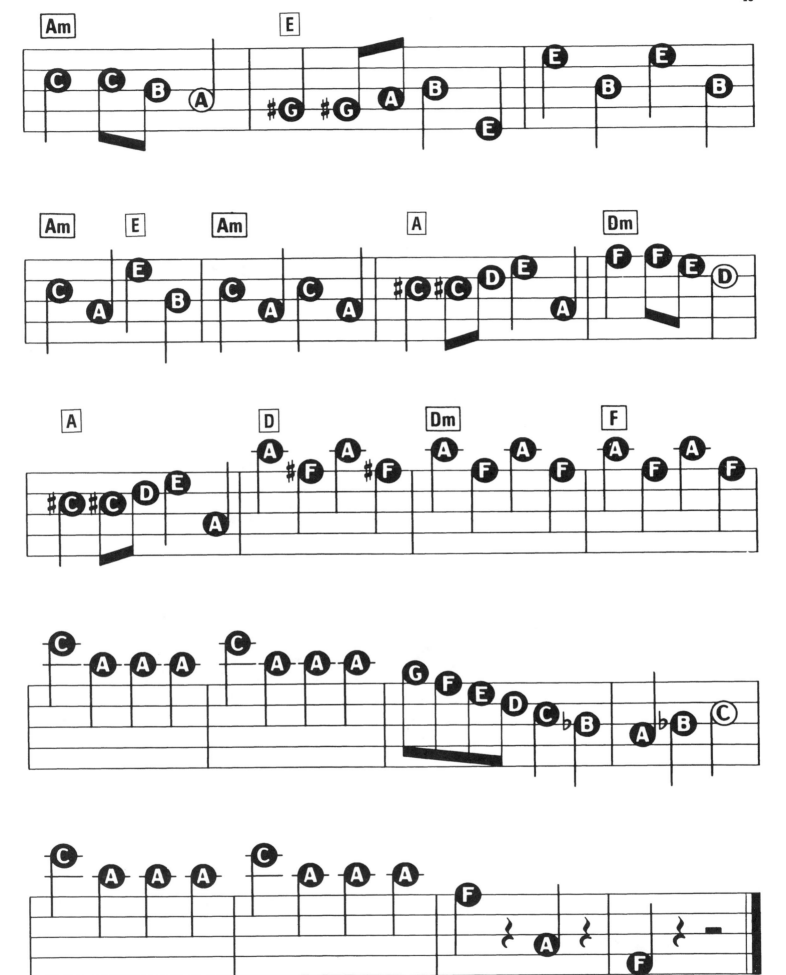

Waltz in A Minor

Registration 8
Rhythm: Waltz

By Frédéric Chopin

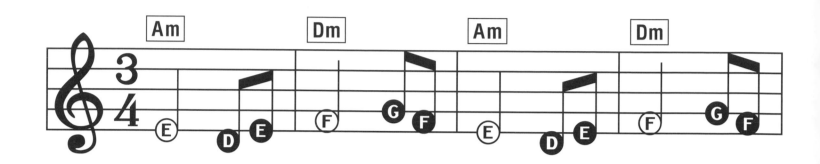

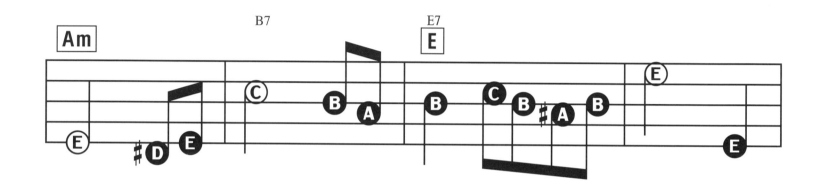

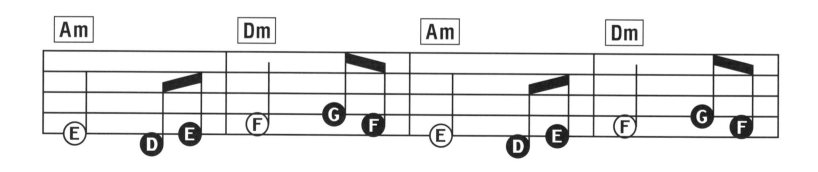

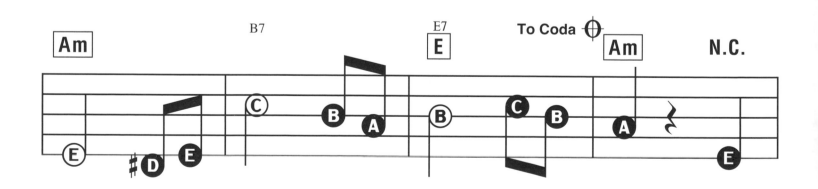

Copyright © 2018 by HAL LEONARD LLC
International Copyright Secured   All Rights Reserved

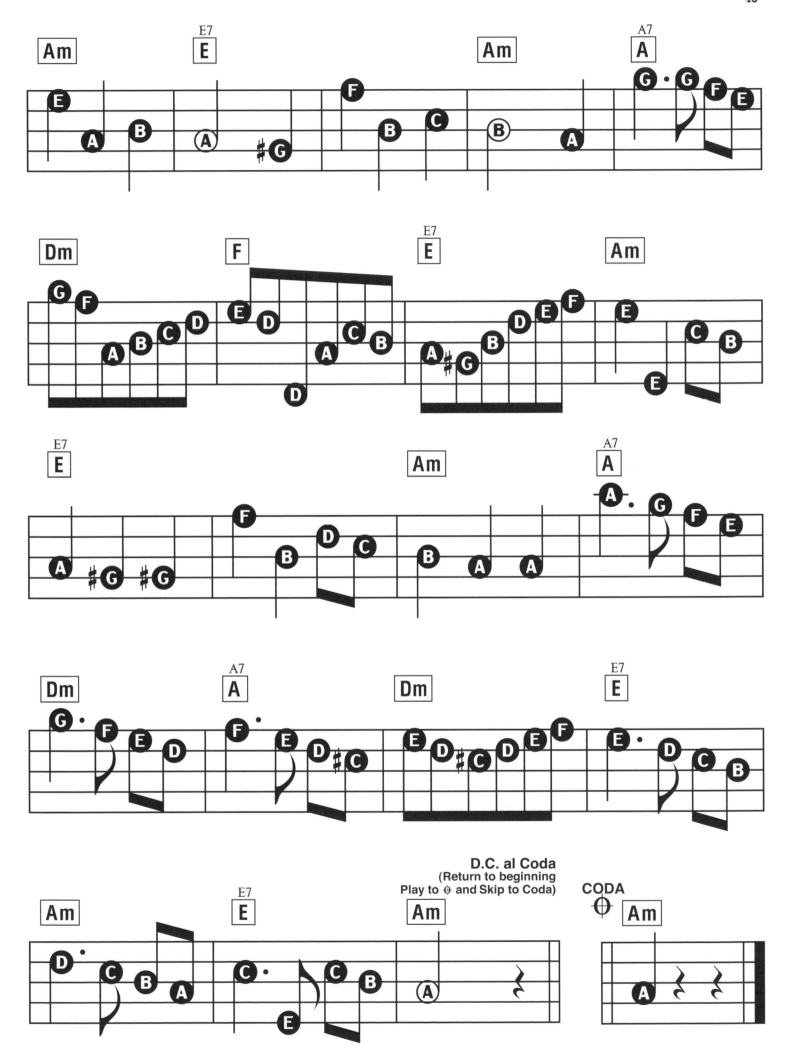

Symphony No. 5 in C Minor
First Movement

Registration 3
Rhythm: None

By Ludwig van Beethoven

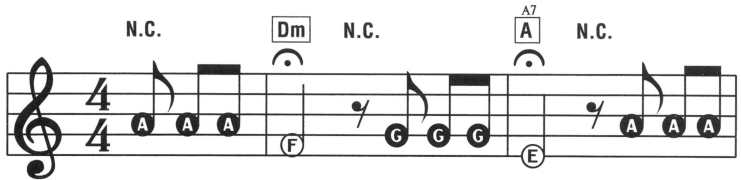

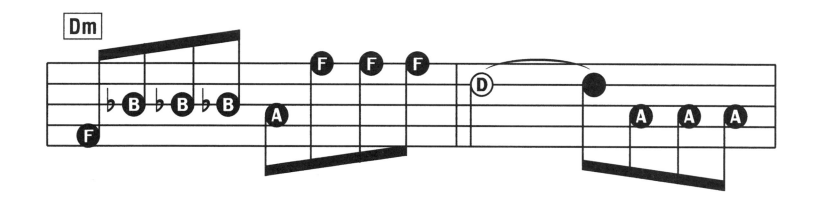

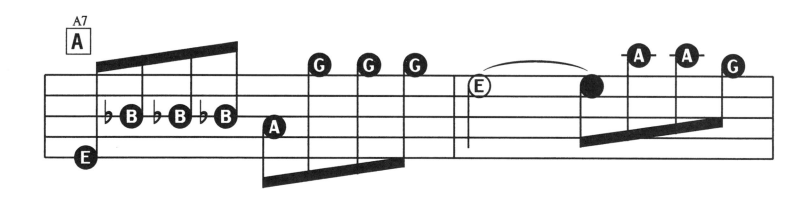

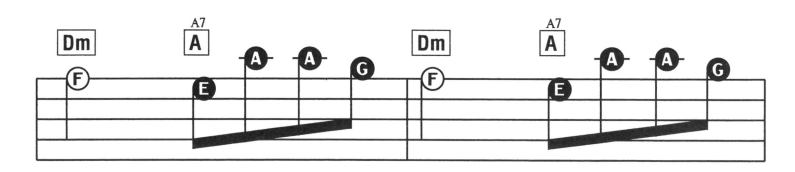

Copyright © 1992 by HAL LEONARD CORPORATION
International Copyright Secured   All Rights Reserved

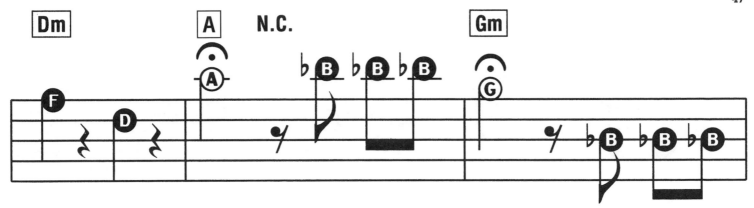

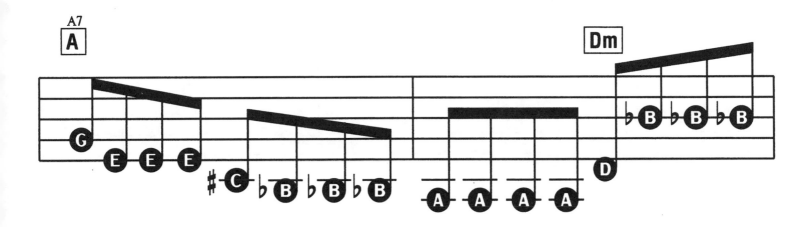

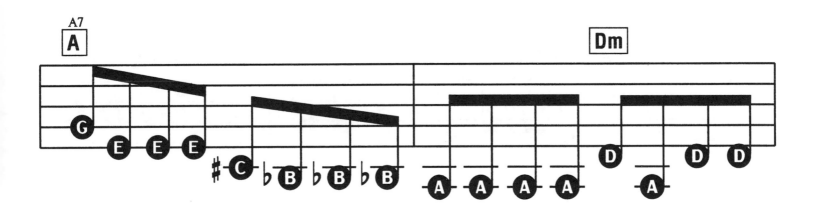

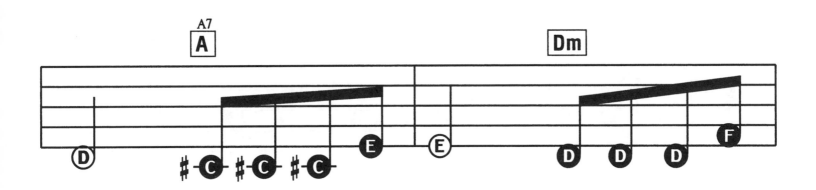

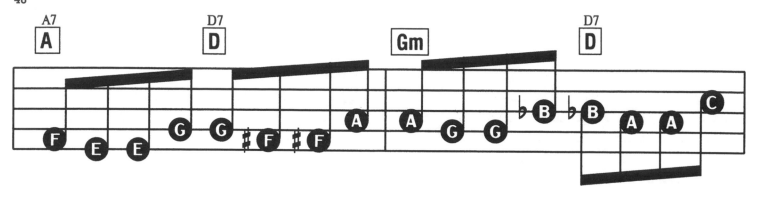

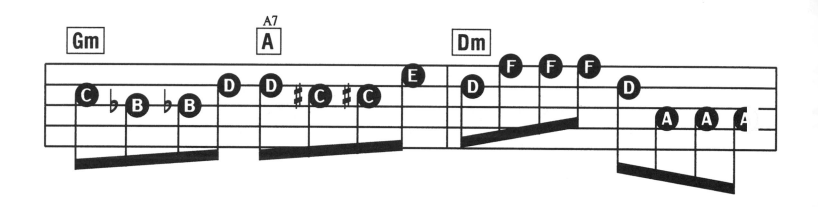

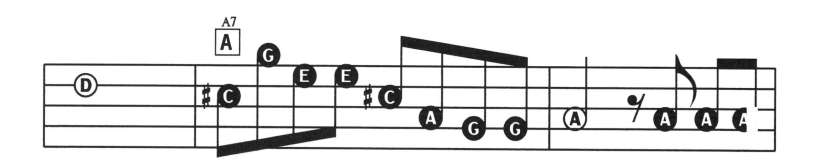